Josephine Pollard, Walter Satterlee

The Decorative Sisters

a modern Ballad

Josephine Pollard, Walter Satterlee

The Decorative Sisters
a modern Ballad

ISBN/EAN: 9783742899811

Manufactured in Europe, USA, Canada, Australia, Japa

Cover: Foto ©Thomas Meinert / pixelio.de

Manufactured and distributed by brebook publishing software
(www.brebook.com)

Josephine Pollard, Walter Satterlee

The Decorative Sisters

THE DECORATIVE Sisters

→ a modern Ballad ←
BY JOSEPHINE POLLARD.

WITH ILLUSTRATIONS BY
WALTER SATTERLEE.

NEW YORK.
ANSON D. F. RANDOLPH & Cº.

THE DECORATIVE SISTERS:

A MODERN BALLAD.

BY

JOSEPHINE POLLARD.

WITH ILLUSTRATIONS BY

WALTER SATTERLEE.

I.

DOROTHEA and Dorinda were two clever English lasses,
  Who lived from London city not a thousand miles away,
Where the buttercups and daisies grew so thick amid the grasses
  In summer-time the ground appeared like one immense bouquet.

II.

Dorothea fed the chickens, and attended to the dairy,
  And in such domestic duties was her happiness complete ;
While Dorinda was within the house a veritable fairy,
  Whose bread and cakes and pies and things were, oh ! so nice to eat.

III.

Their parents were the very, very plainest kind of people,
  Their home an humble cottage, shaded well with English oaks,
And they worshiped in a little church with hardly any steeple,
  And went to bed at nine o'clock like honest country-folks.

·

Dorothea fed the chickens, and attended to the dairy,
And in such domestic duties was her happiness complete;
While Dorinda was within the house a veritable fairy,
Whose bread and cakes and pies and things were, oh! so nice to eat.

IV.

One day as Dorothea, with her sleeves rolled up, was busy
   In the milk-house, singing as she skimmed the ivory-tinted cream,
She heard a step beside her and immediately grew dizzy,
   And, as any other woman would, she gave a little scream.

V.

He said—it was a man, of course!—"I humbly beg your pardon
   For such a bold intrusion"—here he made a bow grotesque—
But I am an artist, madam, and would like to sketch your garden,
   And the pastoral scenes about me—so intensely picturesque!"

VI.

Dorothea stood a moment in a roseate reflection,
   While the artist was preparing his umbrella to unfurl,
To herself she softly whispered, "I have surely no objection;"
   To himself he softly whispered, "What a very lovely girl!"

•

One day as Dorothea, with her sleeves
    rolled up, was busy

  In the milk-house, singing as she
    skimmed the ivory-tinted cream,

She heard a step beside her and im-
    mediately grew dizzy,

  And, as any other woman would,
    she gave a little scream.

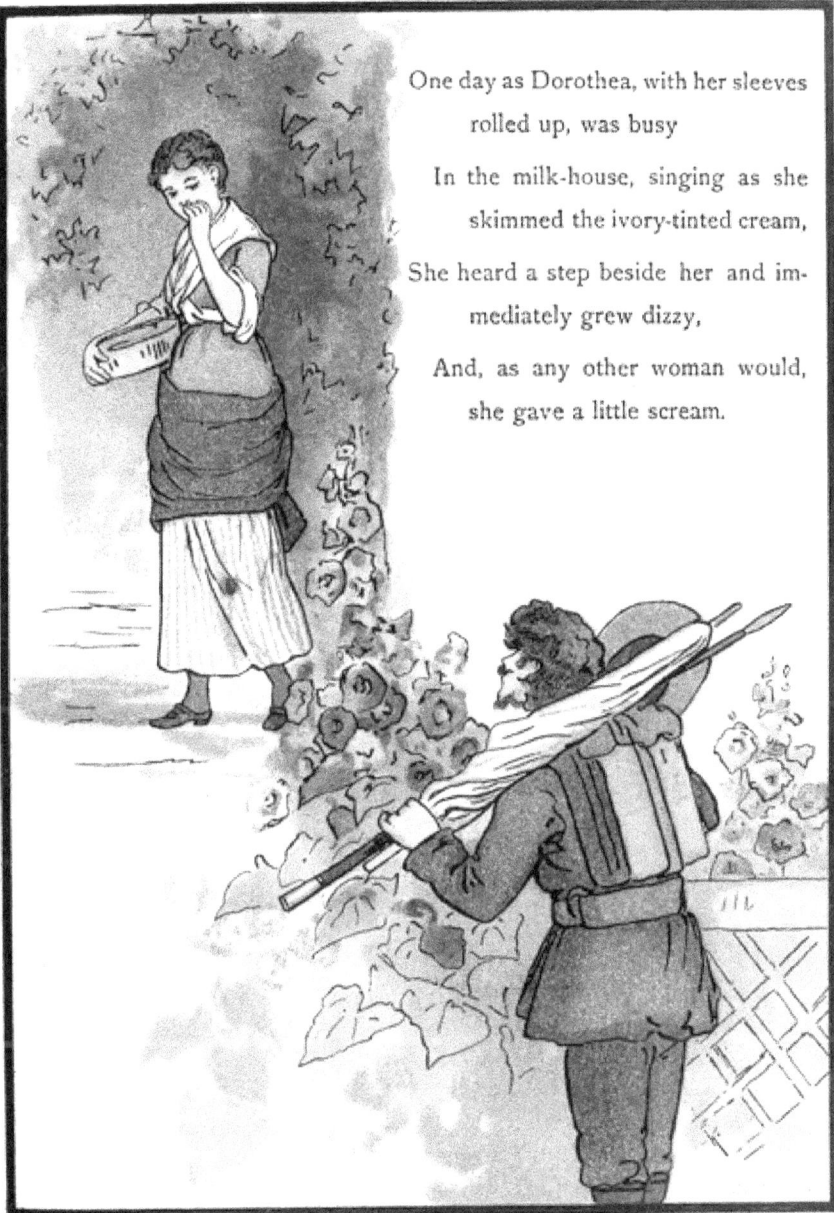

VII.

"That attitude! ah, such repose!" then all at once he missed her,
   For Dorothea never having seen his like before,
Was not a little flustered, and ran in to tell her sister,
   And both together watched him from behind the kitchen-door.

VIII.

'Twas overhung with pretty vines that made a wild endeavor
   To hide the modest maidens well behind their leafy screen,
But the frame-work only made the picture handsomer than ever,
   And added what the artist needed to perfect the scene.

IX.

When he began his sketches, Dorothea and Dorinda
   Recovered from their shyness—he was very sure they would—
And looking slyly at them in a way they could not hinder,
   The artist made a picture of them both just as they stood.

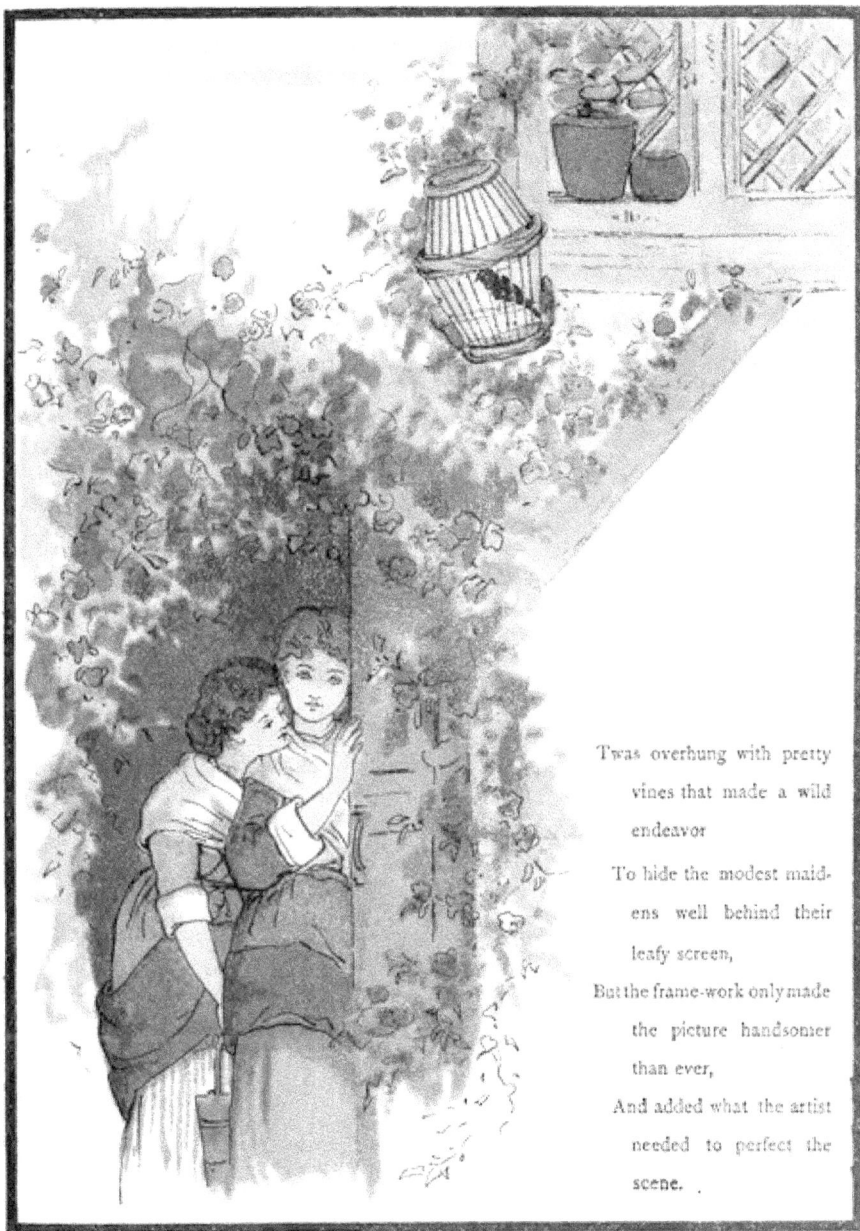

'Twas overhung with pretty
vines that made a wild
endeavor
To hide the modest maid-
ens well behind their
leafy screen,
But the frame-work only made
the picture handsomer
than ever,
And added what the artist
needed to perfect the
scene.

X.

And then he showed it to them. They, astonished and delighted,
  Made haste to let their parents share their joy, you may suppose,
And the old folks smiling pleasantly most cordially invited
  The artist to remain with them what length of time he chose.

And then he showed it to them. They, astonished and delighted,
Made haste to let their parent share their joy, you may suppose,
And the old folks smiling pleasantly most cordially invited
The artist to remain with them what length of time he chose.

XI.

He lingered through the summer, and the autumn, for the weather
  Was delightful, and he really had no yearning to depart ;
Dorothea and Dorinda were his pupils, and together
  They wandered through the labyrinths of Decorative Art.

He lingered through the summer, and the
autumn, for the weather

Was delightful, and he really had no yearning to depart;

Dorothea and Dorinda were his pupils, and
together

They wandered through the labyrinths of
Decorative Art.

XII.

They decorated pots and pans—whate'er the house afforded ;
　They daubed the mirror over with some intricate design ;
And rummaged through the garret, where all sorts of things were hoarded,
　And sat before an ugly plaque as if it were a shrine.

They decorated pots and pans—whate'er the house afforded;

They daubed the mirror over with some intricate design;

And rummaged through the garret, where all sorts of things were hoarded,

And sat before an ugly plaque as if it were a shrine.

XIII.

Dorothea was no longer interested in the churning,
  Her mother made the butter, and her father milked the cows ;
While Dorinda not discerning that the bread and cakes were burning,
  Would pose in languid attitudes with elevated brows.

XIV.

Then naught would do but they must go to London for a season,
  To see the sights, and note the styles, and learn each pretty phrase
Which chanced to be in fashion. You'd have thought they'd lost their reason,
  Had you happened to observe the two on their Æsthetic craze.

●

Dorothea was no longer interested in the
  churning,
  Her mother made the butter, and her father
    milked the cows;
While Dorinda not discerning that the bread
  and cakes were burning,
  Would pose in languid attitudes with ele-
    vated brows.

Then naught would do but they must go to
  London for a season,
  To see the sights, and note the styles, and
    learn each pretty phrase
Which chanced to be in fashion.   You'd have
  thought they'd lost their reason
  Had you happened to observe the two on
    their Æsthetic craze.

XV.

They wore the queerest dresses, and the most outlandish bonnets,
   More ancient than their manners, which were altogether new ;
And their language ! You would never find it in the choicest sonnets,
   'Twas too sumptuously-sumptuous—too awfully too-too !

XVI.

They would gaze upon a lily so "unutterably utter,"
   With eyes distended wide as if the blossom they'd devour ;
'Twas easy to believe they had relinquished bread and butter,
   And really lived on nothing more substantial than a flower.

They would gaze upon a lily, so "un-
    utterably utter,"
  With eyes distended wide as if the
    blossom they'd devour;
'Twas easy to believe they had relin-
    quished bread and butter,
  And really lived on nothing more sub-
    stantial than a flower.

XVII.

The hollyhock was "sweetly sweet," a "lovely-love" the daisy,
Each *shibboleth* the sisters would delightedly repeat,
While a stork upon a spindle-shank would drive them nearly crazy,
And zig-zag lines of crewel-work quite take them off their feet.

XVIII.

They would start with joy ecstatic to behold a peacock's feather;
A cobweb in a corner would occasion wild delight;
And if they saw a sunflower they would clasp their hands together,
And stand amazed as if it were a most enchanting sight.

XIX.

Returning to their country home, these maidens so Æsthetic
Remodeled all the dishes that were on the pantry shelves,
And laid hands upon their mother, and their father so athletic,
And dressed them up so strangely that they hardly knew themselves.

XX.

They went to church on Sunday and surprised the congregation;
The little boys were much amused, the older folks perplexed,
And the minister, who smiled at first, then frowned disapprobation,
Was bothered with his sermon, and kept wandering from the text.

XXI.

For a sight so "utterly utter" was a novel exhibition,
Distracting to the preacher and distracting to the pews,
But the Decorative Sisters were well pleased with their position
And felt 'twas an occasion too "sweetly sweet" to lose.

XXII.

Dorothea watched the pastor with expression most adoring,
While Dorinda fixed her eyes upon a region far away,
But came to earth again when she caught her father snoring,
And gave him such a pinching that he yelled to her dismay.

The hollyhock was "sweetly sweet," a "lovely-
love" the daisy;
Each *shibboleth* the sisters would delightedly
repeat,
While a stork upon a spindle-shank would drive
them nearly crazy,
And zig-zag lines of crewel-work quite take
them off their feet.

They would stare with joy ecstatic to behold a
peacock's feather;
A cobweb in a corner would occasion wild delight;
And if they saw a sunflower they would clasp
their hands together,
And stand amazed as if it were a most enchanting sight.

Returning to their country home, these
maidens so Æsthetic

Remodeled all the dishes that were on
the pantry shelves,

And laid hands upon their mother, and
their father so athletic,

And dressed them up so strangely that
they hardly knew themselves.

They went to church on Sunday and
surprised the congregation ;

The little boys were much aroused,
the older folks perplexed,

And the minister, who smiled at first,
then frowned disapprobation,

Was bothered with his sermon, and
kept wandering from the text.

For a sight so "utterly utter" was a novel
    exhibition,
  Distracting to the preacher and distract-
    ing to the pews,
But the Decorative Sisters were well pleased
    with their position
  And felt 'twas an occasion too "sweetly
    sweet" to lose.

XXIII.

Dorinda took a lily ; Dorothea took a daisy
  As her emblem ; and were thus adorned whenever they went out,
And the village folks, so ignorant ! declared they must be crazy,
  Or the silliest of the silly—which you'll not pretend to doubt.

XXIV.

The Decorative Sisters were so mystically mystic—
  So whimsically whimsey—so intensively intense—
That those who did not know 'twas Æsthetic and Artistic,
  Would surely think that neither had a grain of common sense.

The Decorative Sisters were so mystically
  mystic,—

So whimsically whimsey—so intense-
  ively intense,—

That those who did not know 'twas Æsthetic and Artistic,

Would surely think that neither had a
  grain of common sense.

XXV.

Dorinda wed an artist—and 'twas not the least surprising
    That he used her as a model—for she had a pretty shape—
And so many hours daily was she attitudinizing,
    That she wearied of it truly, and would fain have made escape.

XXVI.

" I've just received an order for a high-art window curtain,"
    Her husband would remark to her with customary smile,
" And you will have to pose for me, Dorinda, that is certain,
    Your costume a la *Grecque*, with hair in corresponding style."

XXVII.

She posed for screens and portieres—she held the fateful lily—
    In tragedy or comedy, whate'er the mood might be,
No matter how she felt herself, 'twas always willy-nilly,
    And how to keep from posing was a poser as you see.

XXVIII.

She wished to be a model wife, but not in artist-fashion ;
    Her "utter-utter" weariness of posturing was such
That her love of the Æsthetic soon became a worn-out passion,
    And Dorinda found it hard to rave and rhapsodize so much.

.

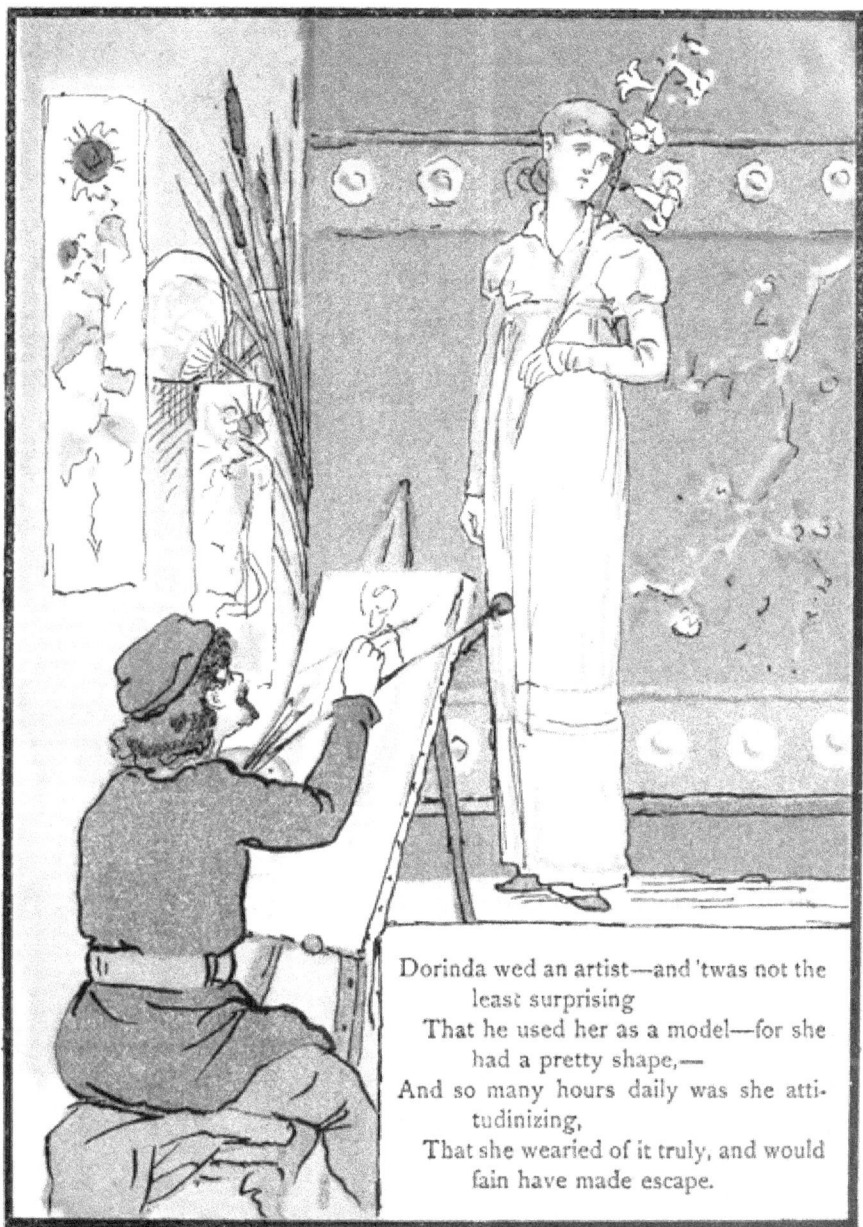

Dorinda wed an artist—and 'twas not the
    least surprising
  That he used her as a model—for she
    had a pretty shape,—
And so many hours daily was she atti-
    tudinizing,
  That she wearied of it truly, and would
    fain have made escape.

XXIX.

She longed to be away from all the crowded city places,
  Away from all the high-art shows where heartlessness prevailed,
Away from all the idiotic genuflexions and grimaces
  That seemed so very silly, now her interest had failed.

XXX.

She longed to be among the fields where daisies starred the grasses;
  She longed to see her early home beneath the English oaks,
And in her dreams she'd visions of the simple little lasses
  Who went to bed at nine o'clock like honest country-folks.

She longed to be among the fields
    where daisies starred the
    grasses ;
She longed to see her early
    home beneath the English
    oaks,
And in her dreams she'd visions
    of the simple little lasses
Who went to bed at nine o'clock
    like honest country-folks.

XXXI.

Dorothea wed a farmer, one who long had loved her truly,
  And though not at all Æsthetic, thought the maiden "sweetly sweet,"
And having told his passion like an honest fellow, duly
  With decorum laid his fortunes at her Decorative feet.

XXXII.

At first, I must confess it, she'd a certain high-art notion
  'Twould be to her advantage rustic lovers to discard,
But underneath her bodice was a terrible commotion
  That let her know the sacrifice would be extremely hard.

XXXIII.

And so she listened to her heart which strove to guide her rightly,
  And when before the altar said with emphasis " I will!"—
And in her pretty cottage home goes singing ever brightly,
  While the kitchen and the dairy give fresh tokens of her skill.

Dorothea wed a farmer, one who long
    had loved her truly,
  And though not at all Æsthetic,
    thought the maiden "sweetly
    sweet,"
And having told his passion like an
    honest fellow, duly
  With decorum laid his fortunes at
    her Decorative feet.

XXXIV.

If you should ever meet her you would smile at the idea
  Of her being "utterly utter" or in any way intense,
For a plain good-natured farmer's wife is Mistress Dorothea,
  Who has a reputation for uncommon common-sense.

XXXV.

And in the pleasant summer-time when daisies are in blossom,
  And hollyhocks and roses stand in luminous array,
Dorinda walks among them with white lilies in her bosom,
  With slow and weary footsteps, looking pale and wan as they.

XXXVI.

As the Decorative Sisters wander arm in arm together,
  And their maiden meditations and absurdities review,
A single glance at them, I'm sure, will soon convince you whether
  Dorothea or Dorinda is the happier of the two.

As the Decorative Sisters wander arm
in arm together,
And their maiden meditations and
absurdities review,
A single glance at them, I'm sure, will
soon convince you whether
Dorothea or Dorinda is the happier of the two.

Drawn on Stone & Printed
by
WEMPLE & COMPANY.
ART LITHOGRAPHERS.
New York

Illustrated by

Walter Satterlee.